THE ART OF ACCELERATED LEARNING

PROVEN SCIENTIFIC STRATEGIES FOR SPEED READING, FASTER LEARNING AND UNLOCKING YOUR FULL POTENTIAL

SELENA WATTS

© **Copyright Wryting ltd 2021 - All rights reserved.**

The content contained within this book may not be reproduced, duplicated or transmitted without direct written permission from the author or the publisher.

Under no circumstances will any blame or legal responsibility be held against the publisher, or author, for any damages, reparation, or monetary loss due to the information contained within this book, either directly or indirectly.

Legal Notice:

This book is copyright protected. It is only for personal use. You cannot amend, distribute, sell, use, quote or paraphrase any part, or the content within this book, without the consent of the author or publisher.

Disclaimer Notice:

Please note the information contained within this document is for educational and entertainment purposes only. All effort has been executed to present accurate, up to date, reliable, complete information. No warranties of any kind are declared or implied. Readers acknowledge that the author is not engaged in the rendering of legal, financial, medical or professional advice. The content within this book has been derived from various sources. Please consult a licensed professional before attempting any techniques outlined in this book.

By reading this document, the reader agrees that under no circumstances is the author responsible for any losses, direct or indirect, that are incurred as a result of the use of the information contained within this document, including, but not limited to, errors, omissions, or inaccuracies.

CONTENTS

Introduction	5
1. Accelerated Learning: What You Need to Know	11
2. Let's Dig in	28
3. Speed Your Read	44
4. Speed Reading and Retaining Information	59
5. Integrating Ideas	80
6. Maintain Your Brain	92
Conclusion	111
References	119

These amazing resources include:

- Understanding your learning style and reading speed.
- High-quality items that you can use to help you get the most from your studying.
- Where you can obtain really high quality online learning.

The last thing we want is for your learning to be less than perfect because you weren't as prepared as you could have been.

To receive your essential 5-point learning checklist, simply scan the QR code below:

INTRODUCTION

"School days are the best days of your life" said every parent as every child rolled their eyes! Who on Earth would believe that having your head stuck in textbooks is better than going to work and getting paid? I was never the brightest and my head was probably stuck in those books for longer than others. While it was a little late to help my school days, accelerated learning has certainly made my adult learning experiences more productive.

Accelerated learning sounds like an unattainable dream come true. Imagine walking around, looking at information, and just soaking everything up like a sponge. If knowledge is power, I should be the king of the world. The concept of accelerated learning reminds me of a cartoon I watched when I was a teenager, where the main character tried to learn French by listening to a recording of the language while sleeping. However, that night, the recording got stuck on a certain phrase, and when he woke up, that was all he could say. Luckily for him, that phrase was the correct answer to every question he was asked that day, including the question of the meaning of life, so he became incredibly famous and successful. That kind of surrealistic success only exists in imaginative cartoons, but we try to realise it for ourselves as far as our minds are rationally able to.

This image below reminds me of the centuries-old story of ol' Sisyphus, the mythical king of Corinth, and the punishment he received for being a deceitful and egotistical idiot. For all eternity, he was given the punishment of pushing a massive boulder up a sizable hill and watching it roll down just before it reached the top. After experiencing this agonizing frustration, he had to roll it up again, and again, and again. Please keep in mind that this is me hyperbolising and enjoying it immensely, but that's how I felt when I had to study in school. That is also why I procrastinated every single time and tried to cram in as much information as I could the morning before a big test. Why is it that when you need to study, absorb, retain, and comprehend, it suddenly becomes so hard?

There was, of course, also the living, breathing stereotype, which happened to be embodied in one of my friends, of a person who would spend hours and hours memorising schoolwork. She would then come to school the next day telling everyone that she did not study *even one single word* and that she was going to fail. Ironically, both of our studying methods yielded similar results in the end. Ultimately, I think that both these methods—the ultra-time-consuming memorization technique and the inability to concentrate, thus leading to procrastination technique—are two of the deeply flawed methods that accelerated learning aims to improve upon, if not eradicate completely.

The concept of accelerated learning was originally developed for the classroom to provide a space for students, who have different ways of conceiving ideas and processing information, to get a chance at grasping concepts in their own unique way. However, this concept has expanded and developed into methods and practices that can also be used by adult individuals and self-learners to improve any part of their lives or lifestyles. It is also based on the ideas that intelligence is a more diverse concept than once believed and that learning techniques should be adapted to provide a broader support system for more efficient learning outcomes.

I consider myself to be in a cool position, because I am both an educator and a learner. My first three books, *Teaching Yourself to Teach*, *Teaching Online* and *Creating Courses Online* have all been from the point of view of the educator. I am also an avid reader, but often find I spend more time reading lesson plans than I do my favourite book. So, this book is going to be aimed at learners, whether you enjoy reading the latest research, taking short courses, or you are studying for a new career.

Interest in accelerated learning has been speedily growing in the educational sector, and there is now a demand for this learning method, specifically for short-term courses that require extensive study and retention abilities within a short period. The method of accelerated learning has also caught the eye of higher education. The successful implementation of accelerated learning in short courses and other curricula is intended to allow institutions to present courses in a compressed format, which will save them time and money. However, this implementation process is currently incomplete, as more research needs to be conducted.

Speed reading is a product of accelerated learning that has been a focal point of research and discussion. The idea of speed reading is that an individual should be able to drastically increase their reading speed by using specific techniques and mental discipline. This also brings the concept of reading versus the retention of information into focus, as it is natural to wonder if information that is read at an increased speed is as effectively retained in the mind as when an individual is reading at a slower speed. I mean, the whole point of speed reading must be that the reader grasps some of the information, right? That's going to be part of the detailed discussion in this book.

This book follows a specific formula, which starts with the discussion of accelerated learning. This is to create a canvas with a background that you can use to understand all the aspects of speed reading. Later in the book, you will also learn how you can integrate basic accelerated learning techniques to enhance speed reading and to create a peaceful space where the mind can be conditioned for improved speed reading. The final part of the book takes a turn that focuses on brain health and how, from a lifestyle perspective, you can help your brain become a super-brain with minimal effort. When you reach the end, you should feel ready to speed read an encyclopedia, and you'll even have all the tools and information to do so!

WARNING: Re-reading this book may result in spontaneous speed reading.

1

ACCELERATED LEARNING: WHAT YOU NEED TO KNOW

Accelerated learning has been around for quite a while, though it still seems to be relatively unknown and seen as a niche subject by most people who are not part of the academic or educational sphere. This learning type or method is born from the idea that traditional learning styles are not as effective as they should be. It is also known as "biologically accelerated learning," and its aim is to use in-depth knowledge of how the human mind functions to improve and customise the learning process for faster and more efficient results.

The original focus in the study of accelerated learning was on teenagers and young adults, but the concept has since been developed and diversified to provide tools for adults and younger children. Although the pupil's age may change, many of the principles hold the same level of relevance, as there are specific processes in the mind, like methods of observation, that remain more or less the same as one gets older. To understand how this idea developed, where the need for it came from, and to create a platform from which techniques like speed reading can be contextually understood, we're going to start at the very beginning when the concept of accelerated learning was still a primordial soup in the universe of existing learning practices.

LET'S LOOK AT HISTORY

The first concept of accelerated learning came from the Bulgarian psychiatrist Georgi Lozanov. At this stage, Lozanov named his method "suggestopedia" or "suggestology", and it was initially focused on foreign language acquisition. Like many psychiatrists, Lozanov focused on the importance of the subconscious mind; according to Lozanov, the subconscious was a key component in the acquisition of new knowledge.

One of the reasons Lozanov developed suggestology was because of his concern that existing learning styles and methods would not be able to keep up with rapidly advancing technology, which he believed could affect the learner on many levels. He believed that a learner's spiritual, mental, and physical health was important for an optimal learning process.

Essentially, accelerated learning started with Lozanov's method of activating the brain's right hemisphere with superliminal instruction (which refers to instruction that occurs above the level of the subconscious mind), which improves the learning process. Examples of superliminal instruction are activities including music, games, roleplay, and art. Lozanov's Suggestology Research Institute was founded in 1966 in Sofia, Bulgaria. Not long after, Accelerated Learning was founded in 1976 in the United States.

After only ten years of research and modification, superliminal instruction and the concept of suggestopedia have morphed into a methodology consisting of a wide range of applicational potential and a multi-method approach that stretches far beyond the practice of language acquisition.

LEARNING STYLES AND STRATEGIES

Everyone who worked their way through school or who deals with people in a working environment has probably noticed that individuals tend to learn and understand things at different speeds, using different methods, and by using different paths of reasoning. A common misconception is that those who acquire knowledge easily through conventional methods are more intelligent than others. This is emphasised by the fact that a class of students get the same learning, the same exam, and different grades—then based on those grades, we might doubt the intelligence of some of those students. But extensive research on this topic has shown that there is a lot more to learning and intelligence than previously thought. This indication toward a broader definition for words like *intelligence* is why accelerated learning adopts a holistic approach that aims to use the "whole" brain, the "whole" individual, and the "whole" environment in the learning process. It is now more commonly known that there are different types of intelligences and that not all of them were utilised in the traditional learning process, which is why the need for an updated learning methodology was identified.

Your dominant learning style will probably be a combination of the following types.

In the center of the learning style spectrum, there are the social versus solitary learning styles. The social temperament is also known as the interpersonal learning style, and interpersonal learners tend to perform well in a social working environment or study setting. If you are a social learner, you understand body language and can sense other people's moods because you are a strong verbal and non-verbal communicator. Your learning environment can be a one-on-one session with another learner or tutor, or it can be in a larger group, as long as the solitary element is excluded. Another aspect that makes learning easier for a social learner in a group setting is if there is a connection or synergy between the members of the group; this can provide a high level of learning satisfaction. A social learner thrives off of exchanging information and receiving feedback on their ideas. When it comes to games and sports, you'll most likely be a board game fan and a team sports player.

Solitary learners are seen as individuals who don't have trouble concentrating in general if they allow themselves to focus on a topic. This is because they need few external stimuli to help them achieve this state: they just need interest and curiosity. Solitary learners are also introspective by nature and will apply this to their learning process. If you are a solitary learner, you'll prefer to study alone or in a solitary setting. Overthinking is probably the most common problem a solitary thinker will experience as they prefer solitude and their own perspective instead of talking to someone about a concept they don't understand.

These two learning styles can also be an indication as to whether a learner is introverted or extroverted, or even if they are an ambivert, having a combination of features of the two. Also, if you think about it, identifying this core characteristic of yourself as a learner is very important when it comes to creating an environment where you can enjoy learning. I am more introverted. So, for example, I would prefer to create my own space and learning process, even if I wouldn't mind discussing ideas in a more social setting after I've made sure that I understand the work myself. So, during the primary learning process, I'm definitely the solitary type. This is a great way to start assessing yourself as a learner. Imagine yourself in both settings with work that is not too easy to grasp. Would you prefer a bustling atmosphere and a group discussion, or would you like your own personal and customisable space?

Next, the outer layers include visual, aural, physical, verbal, and logical learning styles. When it comes to these secondary or outer layers, you don't necessarily associate with only one of these styles, but there can be a dominant style. For example, apart from being a solitary learner, you may be dominant logical, but you are also strong visually and verbally. By looking at each learning style in more detail, you will soon realise that they are actually superpowers in their own right.

Visual

The visual learning style is also called the spatial approach or learning style. If you are visually oriented when it comes to learning, it means that you like to use images, drawings, or to create maps to help you absorb and retain information. If you see information in these formats, you are more likely to remember it, and you can also effectively use imagery to communicate with other people. Imagine the ultimate Pictionary player. It's not an easy game to play—not for me, anyhow. So, if you are a visual learner, you've got my respect! Some interesting facts about spatially oriented learners are that they are more inclined to understand maps and navigate themselves effectively, and they rarely take the wrong turn when they walk out of an elevator. It's so interesting how the elevator fact shows that the visual learner's environment is automatically understood, even from a broader and momentarily unseen context, from a visual perspective that helps them to make the correct choices in this regard.

The visual learner's best tool (and best friend) from a learning perspective is the whiteboard. This is a must-have in any visually oriented individual's learning space, as it can be used over and over to design, draw, map, erase, and repeat. A more up-to-date version of a white board is an iPad with a nifty stylus where a learner can integrate pictures, notes, diagrams, and even the occasional meme or emoji. The sky's the limit.

Logical

A logic is easy to spot, especially if the logical/mathematical style is their dominant learning style. This is because logical learners have an innate ability to identify patterns, and they particularly enjoy assessing situations using logical or mathematical reasoning. It's almost like having a mechanism in your brain that automatically provides evaluations and statistics on everything you encounter and deem worthy for mental processing. It is also no surprise that a logical learner is able to do more complex calculations and that they most likely enjoy working with numbers. It's this ability of assessing and compartmentalising information that helps a logical learner to understand and process information.

The logical learner is one of the darlings of the traditional learning method because of their naturally inclined systematic and procedural behavior. They even have a knack for creating procedures for possible future occurrences, which makes their abilities practical and coveted in a modern society. To understand an idea or concept, a logical learner will often need a practical or statistical example as an illustration, and this is also the way a logical learner will attempt to explain an idea to others. Logical learners have a lot to offer with their highly organised approach to learning and reasoning, but they are also prone to getting stuck, because they don't allow themselves enough context or try to understand the reasoning behind their abilities.

Physical

The physical learning style is also known as the kinesthetic style. If you are kinesthetically oriented, you are much more in touch with your body and with sensory perception. Using your body is something that comes naturally to you, and that is why so many kinesthetic learners are more likely to enjoy exercising or doing some kind of sport. Moving your body helps you to think, and you most likely enjoy activities that involve sensory perception, like working on your flower beds on a Saturday morning.

When it comes to learning, just looking at a picture or map will not satisfy your mind. An ideal activity for a kinesthetic learner is physically demonstrative, like charades. Alternatively, if you need to learn a more complex idea or structure, the ideal solution would be for you to tamper with it yourself, using your hands to take it apart and putting it back together. Nothing will give you more joy than feeling a physical click between your hands and understanding how and why that click just happened. Don't blame physical learners for being restless and fidgety when they need to sit still for an extended period of time listening to someone else talking. They would rather play a physical role in the explanation, demonstration, or process, which would stimulate their minds and help them to learn faster and more efficiently.

Verbal

The verbal learning style, which is also known as the linguistic learning style, works very well if you are also more of a social learner. This is because a visual learner essentially uses speaking and writing as a means to understand new information. Verbal learners are usually skillful with the composition of sentence structure and their language boasts a broad vocabulary. They use these linguistic skills to help them differentiate between ideas that may be similar in some respects and ultimately to understand which aspects in these ideas are different and why. This also makes them very meticulous thinkers and communicators. Some tools verbal learners like to use for learning, sometimes completely spontaneously, are rhymes, tongue-twisters, and their own personalized sayings and phrases.

The best way for a verbal learner to acquire new information and retain this information is to have an animated discussion, listen to a detailed and well-worded lecture, or by reading a text that contains captivating and descriptive language.

Aural

The aural learning style is associated with rhythm and an aptitude for music. Your attention will always be on sounds, background music, rhythm, and even pitch. This can make the acquisition of information more challenging than with the other learning styles, because music is so different from using words, logic, or even to taking a physical approach. It's like speaking a completely different language that is not commonly used in practical situations. When it comes to absorbing new information or ideas, the aural learner has a way of putting these words or sentences in a rhythmic sequence, something that comes naturally. This promotes the retention process as the learner will easily remember the rhythm, which they will associate with the information. Aural learners also have a clear advantage when using specific types of music as a background for studying. Some music promotes an ideal atmosphere for studying, and aural learners benefit from this by being sensitive to the music and the atmosphere it creates. How does it feel walking around with a perpetual rhythm in your head? Just ask an aural learner.

Again, it's perfectly normal for you to connect with more than one learning style. Despite numbers not being my best friend, I know that I prefer a logical approach; I like to have a structure. I just played the worst round of Pictionary with my students today, but as sad as this sounds, I get really excited by a spider diagram with colours. When you start to look at each skill, you will probably find that one will dominate.

Let's take an example—Ikea! You have just bought an Ikea wardrobe. Are you the type of person who will look at the instructions, ask someone to read them to you, or throw them out the window and just start putting pieces together?

WHAT AFFECTS LEARNING?

Based on all the different learning styles we discussed above, there are plenty of aspects that can affect learning, especially if an instructor is trying to teach information to a group of people who have different dominant learning styles. This is why accelerated learning is deemed so important and why it has been developed so extensively. Another way to look at what affects learning, apart from looking at learning styles, is to look at the shift made from traditional learning to accelerated learning and the stark contrast between the two methods. This angle shows you the change in perspective at the philosophical level of educational instruction and learning methodology. There has been a complete change in teaching philosophy, and the new values of accelerated learning makes traditional learning and the environment it creates for learners look hostile and almost criminal.

According to the National Accelerated Learning Network (NALN), there is a distinct and crucial difference between traditional learning methods and accelerated learning, and they have developed a philosophy that compares the most crucial elements of both learning approaches. When looking at these comparisons, accelerated learning appears to be a breath of fresh air and more suited for a postmodern environment. Let's look at some of the key comparisons:

Firstly, one of the key elements that is also described in the history of accelerated learning is the focus on "wholeness," which can be seen as the different components of a learner's mind working together in the learning process. This concept is compared to traditional learning's focus on "separateness," which means that focus is placed on one learning method, one mental process, or one learning style.

Another key idea that integrates with wholeness is how the NALN associates accelerated learning with diversity. This immediately sets the standard to one of inclusivity, acceptance, and individuality. The idea of diversity can be applied in a classroom setting but also from an individual perspective. What this key concept in accelerated learning teaches us is that you need to accept yourself and how your mind works in order for your efforts to be successful. Work with what you've got and use it to your advantage. This is one of the major changes that specialists identified that needed to be made to support effective learning for diverse minds. On the other hand, traditional learning methods promote uniformity, which gets (and got) most of us through the motions during our educational years, but why use this method if a holistic approach has so many more benefits for the learner on the intended and targeted physical, spiritual, and mental levels?

Again, this point links with the next comparison made by the NALN, which is that traditional learning aims to underplay and trivialise the learner and accelerated learning aims to elevate and empower the learner. As an adult learner who wants to use this approach individually, one should also adopt this healthy mindset promoted by accelerated learning. For perfectionists, this is especially difficult, as self-criticism is their mental bread and butter. However, finding the balance is part of the holistic approach that promotes acceptance and builds an optimal learning technique.

Another profound comparison included is that traditional learning is exclusively audio-visual, while accelerated learning focuses on a multi-sensory approach. This goes back to Lezonov's suggestology, and it is a fundamental component of the accelerated learning process that contributes to its success. We will later discuss how creating a multi-sensory environment that you find pleasing can enhance your learning abilities, instead of only reading a text out loud and trying to remember the sound of your own voice. This sensory method allows you to release energy, while traditional learning methods stifle or block energy, causing mental and physical fatigue. While traditional learning is meant to be a process, accelerated learning should be a state of mind.

SO, THEN, WHAT IS ACCELERATED LEARNING?

The best way to describe accelerated learning after discussing all of the former components is that it is a multidimensional approach that aims to place a learner in direct control of their learning experience and learning process. This method also aims to provide an atmosphere where learners can absorb information and ultimately retain it in a way that is multisensory. The accelerated learning process aims to help a learner increase their retention and understanding of information in less time, and to also make the experience one that the learner enjoys, as this will add to the value of the learning experience.

Accelerated learning aims to focus on the learner as a whole and how they experience things from a more holistic perspective, instead of only focusing on aspects like concentration and memorisation, for example. It is often referred to as the "whole brain approach". The point is to understand which other contributing factors exist that can be useful in the learning process which have been neglected or deemed unimportant in other learning styles. For example, if an individual attempts to absorb information, which physiological tools can they use to accomplish this, making efficient use of time? These are some of the points we are going to look at further on in the book as well as how you, as an individual, can use them to your advantage.

A final important aspect of accelerated learning that will help us understand its philosophy is that it is based on the principle that a learner is supposed to *create* knowledge, instead of simply absorbing it. Therefore, accelerated learning methods are more focused on activities and interaction using different stimuli, instead of only focusing on a monolithic presentation-based style.

Now that we've waded through a lengthy definition and discussion of accelerated learning and its basics, the next chapter will focus more on practical uses for us as adult individuals and provide some ideas on how you can kick-start your mind holistically.

2

LET'S DIG IN

There is such a big difference between traditional learning and accelerated learning that I can't help but wonder how I would have performed in school if a traditional learning method was traded in for the newer approach. Would I be accepting my Nobel Prize in Medicine or Literature? Maybe not, but I'm sure it would have been more enjoyable as well as beneficial. However, I recognise aspects of it being purposefully incorporated by some of my instructors, which did make their classes a joy to attend as the environment was more comfortable, the instructor was more approachable, and the idea of a "stupid question" didn't exist. In the end, if you realise that you can learn easily and effectively, then learning becomes an activity you enjoy. If I had to start my entire biology curriculum again today, I must say, I don't know if traditional learning would do the trick.

Here's where the practical and functional discussion starts regarding becoming an accelerated learner and an aspiring speed reader. First, we need to look at components that accelerated learners find useful for their learning process and become acquainted with these practices before we move on to an in-depth focus on speed reading. Let's start with the very basics by looking at key ideas you can implement for successful accelerated learning.

KEY IDEAS FOR AN ACCELERATED SELF-LEARNER

When learners have access to an environment where there is a variety of learning options, they are most likely to learn more efficiently whilst enjoying the process of learning. This is why the accelerated learning approach aims to engage learners on multiple levels simultaneously, as it enhances and improves the effects of the learning process. The following principles of accelerated learning were studied due to their relationship with how the mind acquires and retains knowledge. These principles are held in high esteem for their ability to help a learner activate the analytical and emotional brain as well as the conscious and unconscious mind, which leads to the ultimate enhanced learning experience.

Experimentation

Experimentation, here, is used in a broader context, which includes elements of play and a sense of discovery in the experimentation process. If we look at children, it's easy to see how the element of play and experimentation can dramatically increase their learning potential, but as adults, we seem to think that we've outgrown this important tool for efficient learning.

The benefit of incorporating experimentation and play into your learning process is that you take another step toward creating your own learning safe space, where all your thoughts and ideas can be deliberated and pre-tested from within an empowering and creative environment. If, for example, you want to engage in learning and the content is more on the serious side, why not experiment with aspects of it by creating and playing a game and even make it a fun game? After all, it's all in the name of knowledge, and this is one of your personal tools.

How Are Those Feelings?

Never underestimate the power of your emotions, even if you think you have them a hundred percent under control or that they are not specifically relevant in a certain situation. Being mindful of your emotions and treating them as lovingly as your proverbial rose garden will reap great benefits for you as a learner. Emotional states play a central role in efficient learning, and the fact that humans require emotion to learn is a principle of accelerated learning.

Let's look at an uncomplicated example of trying to teach something to a happy child versus a child who is fuming or crying. The happy child will be more emotionally available for new information, while the fuming child will be caught up in their own thoughts and negative feelings and may be reactive instead of being naturally proactive in a learning environment. Imagine your emotions and emotional state as this inner child. If you want to open yourself up to new information with the aim to retain and understand it, your inner child will stand in your way if they are upset or angry. So, it's important to remember to keep that inner child happy when entering your learning space, whether they need a hug, some candy, a few minutes to cool down, or even, if you deem it necessary, a good talking-to.

I have noticed with so many adult learners that they can become confident in a subject, so much so that they can explain concepts to me. But if they are stressed or have too many other things on their mind, it is much harder to demonstrate what they have learnt.

Your Learning Environment

The effect of the learning environment on a learner's abilities is something we have touched on previously in the book, by looking at learner types. Here, the importance of the learning environment as an accelerated learning principle is going to be laid out and discussed in more detail, not in terms of nature, but in terms of necessity and purpose.

A learner's environment can affect their learning abilities on both a conscious and subconscious level. The idea of "environment" can include so many components because of the diversity in learning styles and their connected sensitivities. For example, common environmental factors can include the acoustic quality of a learning environment, the colour of the room, how the space makes the learner feel, and where the learner is placed or places themselves within the learning environment. Some of these factors can easily be traced back to visual, aural, and interpersonal learning styles. There may even be a picture against the wall that has not been placed in the center of the wall, which can irritate the subconscious mind of a logical learner. The possibilities are endless.

Therefore, it is actually easier to create the ideal learning environment for an individual learner, because a group of learners will all have different environmental requirements. If you know what your dominant learning style is, or if you have identified or associated with more than one learning style, you are off to a very good start in creating the ultimate functional learning environment.

Staying Motivated

Motivation from an accelerated learning perspective includes not only being and staying motivated but knowing what motivates you as a learner. This principle focuses on intrinsic motivators like self-confidence, your expectations as a learner, and your desires, instead of taking the old road by primarily focusing on the extrinsic motivators like good grades, academic ranking, and awards.

This is a 'before, during, and after' principle, because becoming an accelerated learner will require motivation, the learning process will require motivation, and going back and doing it again after it may not have been entirely successful the first time will also require motivation.

Intrinsic motivation is the most powerful motivation there is for learning and historically was never used, because of the traditional method's focus on uniformity. Not all learners have the same goals and driving forces, so extrinsic motivators like good grades and the respect that comes with it are what traditional methods promote. The range of intrinsic motivators that exist in learners, due to the scope of individualism, has to be far more sweeping than the few extrinsic motivators used to achieve traditional academic uniformity. Finally, being motivated again comes down to understanding yourself and knowing who you are. From a learning perspective, you can use tools like identifying your learning style along with your temperament and personality to shape and identify your intrinsic motivations. You will know when you've found them when you can stay true to them and they can keep you above board. And, if you don't find these tools immediately, fake it 'til you make it. Remember what the purpose of your learning experience and journey is and try to find a point where you resonate with the subject or its content.

Imagination and Visualisation

This accelerated learning principle focuses on how incorporating visualisation, your imagination, and the use of metaphors can enhance the learning process . The fact that these tools are not only connected to certain learning styles, but that all learners are encouraged to use them, indicates that they are useful tools when creating a "whole" learning experience, even though some learners may be better at using specific tools than others.

In fact, incorporating a tool that is not associated with your learning style at all can provide insight that would otherwise have been lost. For example, a logical learner can gain a lot from taking a step back and visualising the bigger picture of their systematic reasoning process. Although visualisation may not be their strong point, this creates a holistic learning process where retention and comprehension are attained faster and more efficiently.

The Beneficial Act of Suggestion

As another accelerated learning principle, learners need to remember that not everything is set in stone. This principle focuses on the power of suggestion, which can come from the learners themselves or from someone they are interacting with. A common effect of suggestion is for us to develop preconceived notions about things that may not be entirely accurate. These preconceived notions can be self-centered or focused on the learner's worldview and immediate environment. There are two sides to the principle of suggestion that are important to be aware of. It can either enhance the learning process by being open and accepting, or it can limit and slow down the learning process by being closed and stubborn. Personal suggestions are also known as beliefs, or "mental models" and they are the catalysts that bring about the positive or negative influence in the learning process.

As a self-learner or an individual learner who wants to utilise accelerated learning, you can use this information for introspective purposes; ensuring that you do not have any misconceptions about yourself or what you are capable of as a learner. If you find that you have beliefs or mental models that are self-limiting, then you can now work toward developing a more learner-friendly perception of yourself, which will ultimately be rewarding. Set out to accomplish tasks successfully and with positivity and remember to give yourself credit.

THE DIFFERENT FORMS OF INTELLIGENCE

There are aspects of the multiple intelligences theory that resemble the different learning styles, most likely because they are so closely related. The theory of multiple intelligences is the brainchild of Dr Howard Gardner, a Harvard professor who published what was seen as a "groundbreaking" study named "Frames of Mind: The Theory of Multiple Intelligences". This research completely changed people's perception of what makes an individual smart or intelligent, as Gardner argued that there are several ways a person can be smart as opposed to the conventional perception of being "IQ" smart. His simplified example is that a student who excels in algebra only has a different type of intelligence than a student who excels in art. Thus, we cannot conclude that one is smarter than the other. Despite Gardner's research, IQ tests are still widely used, and their results are highly valued as they accommodate and support the traditional learning methods that focus on uniformity.

As we mentioned earlier, the idea of accelerated learning not only began to assist language acquisition, but also specifically for instructions and not for self-use. This is where Gardner's research was first implemented by educators who strived to create a more multifaceted method of instruction in order to cater for individuals, instead of maintaining a group mentality. As Gardner is known for saying, all humans are intelligent in some way, but some are intelligent in some areas, and others in other areas. Therefore, this multifaceted approach also targeted individual needs and preferences that may have been neglected under a uniform method. We are seeing this more in the workplace today as employers are starting to appreciate the importance of emotional intelligence, as measured by the emotional quotient (EQ).

Multiple Intelligences

Gardner's eight intelligence types include phrases that sound both familiar and new. The first few can all relate to the learning styles discussed earlier in the book and include verbal-linguistic, logical-mathematical, visual-spatial, physical-kinesthetic, musical-rhythmic, naturalist, interpersonal, and intrapersonal. Interpersonal intelligence has a lot in common with the social learning style, while intrapersonal intelligence has a lot in common with the solitary learning style. Let's run through them swiftly and add some new details that include ideal career choices to put these categories of intelligence into perspective.

Individuals of the verbal-linguistic intelligence type are able to express themselves successfully in several ways, which can take the form of letters, essays, debates, articles, and books. This means that they have no problem stringing a bunch of words together that will be an apt expression of whatever it is they want the audience or reader to know. They are often described as eloquent and known as wordsmiths. Verbal-linguistic types are comfortable as writers, academics, journalists, or working in the media.

Next is the logical-mathematical intelligence type, and we know by now that they are very methodical and, dare I say, unspontaneous. Their ability to reason deductively and inductively and perform complex calculations makes them the perfect candidates for professions such as computer programmers, accountants, mathematicians, and scientists. They are your STEM candidates, and their occupations are always in demand by society and the economy.

The visual-spatials think in pictures and use imagery, so I imagine that colour plays a pivotal role not only in their lives but also in their mood and wellbeing. Imagine placing an individual with visual-spatial intelligence in a room painted with their least-favourite colour—mine is orange. I don't know why; I just find it repulsive. I'd go mad! Visual-spatials are artistically inclined and pay great attention to detail. They can become accomplished photographers, designers, and visual artists.

The physical-kinesthetics like physical movement and even physical manipulation. They are also known to be good with creating things with their hands. These skills stem from a heightened ability to develop muscle memory that enables them to remember, for example, the sequence of dance steps, effective moves in sports, and how to replicate and repeat any move that manipulates the physical body. This intelligence type is highly underrated as it is not as in-demand in our economically oriented society, except when it comes to professional sports. However, an individual of the physical-kinesthetic intelligence type can be a successful mechanical engineer, an accomplished surgeon, or even a professional woodworker.

Next is the musical-rhythmic intelligence type. These individuals don't necessarily play musical instruments, although they have the potential to, but they are affected by music, pitch, and sounds in a different way to others. Individuals with this type of intelligence usually also have a love for music because they are so influenced by it, and they have the potential to become instrumentalists/musicians, composers, conductors, or singers, or even a combination of these, because, as a musician in today's society, being multifaceted is a great asset. Another more modern and often overlooked option for a musical-rhythmic type is sound engineering. Did you think about it? People tend to forget that it's an option because it is not associated with the traditional career choices for music.

The naturalist intelligence type is one we haven't come across in the learning styles. This intelligence type is the one who possesses the green thumb, among other gifts. They are the horse-whisperers among us. These unique individuals feel comfortable in nature, they have a way with animals, and you can give them plants for their birthday because they won't let the plants die. The naturalist intelligence type is particularly sensitive to changes in climate or weather and also to a change in seasons. These individuals will naturally make their way towards positions in forestry, veterinary science, and marine biology. Alternatively, they may farm or run a plant nursery. These individuals can smell the rain coming from a distance and will make an effort to swerve out of the way to save a bird.

Finally, we come to the intra-and-interpersonal intelligences. As previously mentioned, these types appear to resemble the social and solitary learning styles, although they are classified as intelligences and have different names. First, the intrapersonal intelligence type has the ability to conduct deep thinking and effective introspection. They tend to be the sensitive type and need time alone to think and reflect. From this perspective, there is a similarity between the intrapersonal intelligence type and the solitary learning style. Intrapersonals are deep and sensitive thinkers and, therefore, they have a natural aptitude for theology, philosophy, and counseling.

Interpersonal intelligence describes individuals who have effective communication skills and what one would call "people skills." They are associated with an extroverted personality, and this makes them compatible with the social learning style. These individuals thrive in social settings and have a natural affinity for social interaction and understanding social situations. They are your politicians, teachers, coaches, and they can also be counselors. They thrive off the energy of others and have an understanding of communication and relationships.

How the Different Learning Styles Apply

Looking at Gardner's interpretation of the eight intelligences, there appears to be a direct connotation to the learning styles, as some of them even have the same names. Here's the difference: the intelligences are meant to help individuals identify themselves intellectually and realise their strong points and to also create awareness that intelligence is not a monolithic concept. However, the learning styles, which are each specific to an intelligence type and can help you learn more efficiently, are meant to guide an accelerated learning instructor or a self-learner towards creating the ideal learning environment. This is because, even though some learners may have strengths in specific learning styles due to their intelligence types, the benefits of the other learning styles should also be incorporated into the learning environment to create a holistic experience that speeds up learning, comprehension, and retention. And, as mentioned earlier, if you place yourself as a learner into a learning environment that primarily focuses on your learning style but also incorporates other learning styles, you will be able to sharpen intellectual edges and broaden intellectual horizons that you may have not deemed possible or even acknowledged as existing.

Now that we've given accelerated learning a proper run-through, the next chapter is going to focus on a specific skill that originates from the ideological realms of accelerated learning. Yes, we're going to learn how to speed read. Are you ready to stretch your brain?

3

SPEED YOUR READ

When I sat down the other day to read an article about speed reading, the article said "nine-minute read." I couldn't help but wonder if this was in "normal" reading terms or in "speed reading" terms. I soon realized that it was according to normal, or what I would call a common reading speed. So, luckily, the author didn't expect me to speed read their article. But what if I could? Speed reading seems like it would make every aspect of our lives easier.

There are many occupations that require the individual to absorb and retain new information on a daily, monthly, or yearly basis. Medicine and law are only two of these; they are both occupations that consist of and rely on developing data and changes in information or laws and policies. In the medical discipline, this occurs through scientific research, and in law, it happens in court. Each time information is updated or replaced, a medical or legal practitioner needs to revise and retain the new information or "precedents" set by their discipline to efficiently do their jobs. This means that these individuals need the ability to read fast and absorb efficiently for efficient application. Other examples are company leaders who need to stay on top of every department in their enterprise.

Speed reading is not about reading every single word and taking it in at a nano speed like a superhuman. Instead, it's about absorbing the most important details in order to retain a decent summary of the information, especially if you are dealing with a large text. So, speed reading is creating a mental process of rapidly absorbing and recognising sentences or phrases in a text in one go instead of reading it word-for-word. There are a number of reading methods and techniques developed that enable an individual to "speed read." The average individual is able to read 250 words per minute, while some are faster and some are slower. Speed reading claims that you can actually double your reading speed by developing a few techniques.

Another way to identify speed reading is by analyzing trade-offs between comprehension and measures of speed, which means that different speeds and comprehension rates apply to different types of reading and these rates can be improved by practicing.

WHAT'S SPEED READING, AND WHO INVENTED THE IMPOSSIBLE?

Previously, people believed that in order to understand what you read, you need to look at and absorb every single letter on a page. However, experiments conducted by the U.S. Air Force changed this perception and ushered in a new idea of chunked reading, where a reader can still read and comprehend a text without focusing on each word individually. There is no one "inventor" or creator behind speed reading; it seems to be more of an unintended collaborative attempt to improve the reading and retention abilities of the average individual, the basic development of which spanned from the 1940s to the late 1950s.

A multi-dimensional and up-to-date definition of speed reading will indicate a move away from identifying single words and repeating them individually in your head (you're doing it now aren't you?), but rather focusing on absorbing entire phrases, sentences, or even entire pages in one go .

The History

The development and idea of speed reading derives relevance from studies of visual acuity, in which educational specialists and academics were interested in individuals' visual "sharpness." These academics used a machine called a tachistoscope to determine the length of time an individual needs to be visually exposed to or to look at an image before they are able to recognise what it is. They concluded that a small image can be identified if it is displayed for only two milliseconds, which equals one five-hundredth of a second.

The United States Air Force took this idea further by applying it to words, and their studies showed that flashing four words simultaneously at the same speed has the same effect as flashing an image, which means that the reader can recognise0 all four of the words. This is identified as an initial form of "Rapid Serial Visual Presentation," which indicated an improvement potential for reading and processing rates.

Subsequently, the Harvard School of Business produced the first course related to speed-reading in the 1940's, which was based on the discoveries made by the tachistoscope. This course, which was also mainly based on visual processing, utilised film to help readers broaden their area of focus, with the objective of increasing reading speeds. During this decade, the study and practice of increasing one's reading speed became especially popular, and researchers aimed to prove that an individual's average reading speed could be improved by a hundred percent.

The person who coined the term "speed reading" before it became a famous method was Evelyn Wood. Evelyn studied the habits of individuals who have naturally fast reading abilities and consequently developed her own methodology to help people read faster. Her method, called the "Wood Method", was developed from the sweeping motion of the hand when turning a page. She started using her hand as a pacer to aid her in reading more smoothly. The Wood Method was renamed to "Reading Dynamics" in 1958, whereafter Wood started using the phrase "speed reading", which is still used today. Evelyn's research led to many seminars being taught on the campuses of universities across the United States. She also personally taught President John F. Kennedy, who was an accomplished speed reader. Until her passing in 1995, her methods were taught at colleges all over the United States .

Since Wood's passing, speed reading techniques have evolved significantly. For example, reading nowadays is done more frequently on screens than in actual books, so Wood's use of her hand may have been phased, modified, or modernised in that regard, but all developments are still based on the same foundational principles, which also includes visual processing.

Speed Average and Speed Goals

An average speed is something that can be estimated, but a speed goal is more dependent on the individual, their approach, and other factors. We are constantly reminded that speed reading is a multifaceted concept and skill and that it should be approached as such. Therefore, when looking at a speed goal, one should also look at other aspects, like personal development and tools that can assist with personal learning needs.

If you approach speed reading by just trying to read faster, you'll realise that you will start to read slower than you did initially, because you will be so focused on your reading speed that you don't absorb any information, so you need to go back and read it again! That's something that would put me off speed reading immediately, but it's not actually because of the method or the concept, it's because of a faulty approach. It's like when you start playing the piano or when you start riding a bicycle. First, you need to find out where Middle C is, and you need to ride with your training wheels. So, to reach your speed goal is to look at what the average speed is as a guideline and focus on what's actually important—increasing your concentration, as that is the core strength of a speed reader.

Also, let's give "speed goal" a new name, because when you start your speed-reading journey, there is no way for you to know what your speed is going to be when you start practicing and start reading like a pro. Let's call it your ultimate speed comfort zone. This is the zone where you are flying, but it feels right, and you know you are being at your most productive.

You can test yourself and find out what your average reading speed is by locating and using a tester, which you can find online or in most app stores. If you read between two hundred and three hundred words a minute, you are on average, and you know where your journey's starting point is. If you read faster, then that's great! But, if your average is slower at the beginning, it doesn't mean that you don't have the potential to significantly raise that number.

THE SPEED READER'S BASIC LINGO

Seasoned speed readers and speed-reading instructors know their lingo. There are terms you will hear in basically every discussion about speed reading, because these components are crucial to the act and success of speed reading. I saved them for now so I can give you a detailed description and definition of two main terms that are used in speed reading discussions.

Let's see what's so important about these two concepts:

Chunking

When someone talks about chunking, they are referring to a speed reader's ability to read several words at once. Consequently, you need to train your brain to read and understand all of these words at once in order for this exercise to be successful. Chunking is considered a revered speed-reading skill by the gurus. This technique goes all the way back to the studies conducted by the United States Air Force, who took the initiative to move from flashing pictures to flashing four words together in the timespan of two milliseconds to see if individuals could read and retain the information. Now, our chunking gurus have implemented and perfected this technique and recommend it to any aspiring speed reader.

According to your everyday speed reader who chooses the chunking method, it is more time-efficient and practical to read and comprehend a bunch of words in a sentence at once than trying to read and understand the whole sentence. However, I assume the trick here is identifying the words that contain the essential meaning or essence of the sentence, which is something your brain learns to do. When you piece together these chunks skillfully, you will reach a picture of the main text, which is what you want to achieve as a speed reader. Amateur chunkers start at a mere two words at a time and then gradually move up to five. Advanced chunkers aim for five or more, but they still need to focus on quality. Chunking can be combined with other speed-reading methods and techniques and is especially useful when added to your speed-reading basics, which we will be discussing below.

Subvocalisation

Subvocalisation is also known, from a more scientific perspective, as "auditory reassurance". It is a habit that most readers have that comes from the way we were taught to read as children. Were you also asked to read out loud in the classroom a few times? I was, and I was always very nervous of making mistakes when reading out loud. You know you would do anything so that the teacher didn't catch your eye. At that point, it was the teacher's way of measuring your reading abilities, but at the same time, you acquired this habit of "reading out loud" in your mind, even if you're not reading out loud with your voice. Subvocalisation is considered an obstacle for speed readers, because it has been proven to slow down reading speed, even though it enhances the comprehension and retention of information. Although speed readers would want to minimise this habit as far as possible, getting rid of the habit completely is not a possibility; it's almost as if it's hardwired into our minds .

As your ability to read progresses and improves, the full use of subvocalisation is not required anymore, but we still do it out of habit. It is a comfortable support system to fall back onto if your mind needs to verify information you've just read. There are instances, though, when you don't use subvocalisation (or don't have to), because what you are reading is so simple and easy for the mind to grasp. An example is traffic signs at the side of the road or "words" that consist of digits, like dates. However, if you are like me, you may experience moods where you tend to vocalise everything you see out loud, even if there are no words involved.

SPEED READING METHODS

The three speed reading methods below should not be seen as separate methods but as a combined and integrated way of practicing mindful reading. They are the most basic techniques that start from choosing where to sit and progress to how to train yourself in following words on the page or screen. See these methods as the three cornerstones of speed reading that you can build on to develop your own individual style and technique that works best for you.

Basic

Start basic and start simple. Get into the groove, even if you don't have a lot of time. Successful speed reading is all about teaching your mind to multitask, which requires your mind to actively do some things and actively refrain from doing other things. So, the basic method basically focuses on finding your space.

Choose an environment where you can focus your mind, even if it is under your desk in your office, where your boss can't see you. Breathe, and make sure that you have the resources for breathing. Try not to sit in a stuffy area, as your brain will need oxygen to focus. If you wear glasses, make sure that you are wearing them, and also make sure that you have proper lighting, as these small details all affect your brain's ability and agility.

Skimming

Skimming is where we move on to the reading material. Skimming is your most basic speed-reading method, and you may have used it often before when looking for a single detail on a page. However, for speed reading, skimming needs to be implemented more intensively and with more concentration. What you need to do is search visually for the main clues and cues on the page that will provide you with the text's main idea. The standard reading rate for comprehension is 200-230 wpm (words per minute), but skimming requires it to be about 700 wpm. This means that you will be skipping a lot of words while looking for the important ones at the same time. If the text has a title, that can be helpful, as it can give you an indication of what to skim for.

A skimming method that is used by individuals who work with online texts involves identifying parts of the text that appear to be less important or relevant and only focusing on the relevant parts. This skimming method, although not recently invented, has grown in popularity due to its compatibility with the way web content is written. Pro tip: speed readers recommend combining chunking and skimming to fire up your reading speed.

Meta-Guiding

Meta-guiding sounds much more complicated than the previous methods, but it is actually quite simple and very helpful if you find that it works for you. This method goes back to the Wood Method we discussed earlier in the chapter, as it involves using your hand or finger to guide your eye across the page or screen. You can even use a pen, and when you are reading from a desktop computer screen and your arm is getting tired, you can use your cursor by controlling the mouse. You will need to teach your eye not to focus on the guiding instrument but on the words that follow directly behind it. You can also use the guiding instrument as a pacing tool to train your eyes to read faster as you become accustomed to it.

There are also claims by speed reading instructors that if you use an instrument to guide your eye in terms of direction and speed, this can reduce your urge to subvocalise each word, because you are more concerned with keeping up with that pen while understanding what you read at the same time. It's that mental multitasking at work again.

HOW VIABLE IS SPEED READING?

Although there are a lot of individuals who use speed reading and teach speed reading, there are also the doubters who say that speed reading is a hoax. As part of our journey through all the components of accelerated learning and speed reading, this is also an important topic to address, so that we can understand why some people rave about this method and why others call it unattainable. I suspect that it has a lot to do with the expectations of the individual, their patience when it comes to developing this skill, and how much they know about speed reading and the rich background one actually needs to be in touch with to make it work for you.

Because of everything we've read previously in the book about how individuals can differ in terms of the type of intelligence they may have and how learning styles apply to these types, it's easy to see that teaching speed reading or acquiring the skill of speed reading is not a monolithic process that will work the same for everyone.

There have been scientific studies conducted on the topic of speed reading with the aim of debunking the method, but what was achieved was that speed readers have been enabled to differentiate between a reasonable and realistic reading speed as opposed to an unrealistic and unattainable speed. This has now been backed by research, which means that there is a lot more concrete evidence to prove that speed reading is viable and attainable, but not every individual will be able to reach the same levels.

Therefore, it is important that we approach this skill with sufficient knowledge about its background and about our mental and learning strengths that can help us develop speed reading skills. Be prepared and be proactive, and you will reap the rewards.

4

SPEED READING AND RETAINING INFORMATION

The reason we would think about or consider developing speed reading skills is definitely not to skim a page and then stare straight ahead, mouth wide open, with our brains in the shape of question marks. It is important actually to be able to remember or recall what we've read so speedily after conducting this method on a piece of text or literature. So, when in the speed reading process should we start to be concerned about retention? Also, are retention and comprehension the same thing? Does the comprehension of a text mean that you will remember enough of it to efficiently repeat the information to someone else? These are fascinating questions.

We know by now that we can scan a page at lightning speed, but this doesn't mean that we will understand or remember anything written on it. We've also previously discussed that to improve our reading speed, we need to reduce subvocalisation; however, this will affect our ability to retain and comprehend the information, which again defeats the purpose.

IN THE END, READING IS ABOUT RETAINING

It's important to acknowledge that speed reading is not going to work on all types of literature and texts, so one needs to choose wisely when it comes to applying this method. What I mean is that speed reading will defeat the purpose of reading a complicated scientific report or legal document, even if you don't have enough time to give it the attention it needs. If you are looking for specific information in such a document and you know what it is, then you can use speed reading techniques like skimming to locate the information. However, if you want to assess or understand the content of a complicated or technical document, speed reading may not be the most prudent choice. I wouldn't speed read the mortgage for my house!

For complete memorisation, a slower reading speed will be required, but if you don't need to remember something word-for-word, speed reading can work, if the content is not too technical. Speed reading can also be used to get the "gist" of a text, even if it contains a lot of detail. A "gist" refers to the main idea of a text or a piece of literature, so it doesn't require the memorisation of specific phrases or sentences.

Speed reading is successful, not if an impossible reading speed is reached, but when an increased speed is reached, combined with retention and comprehension.

SPEED READING'S EFFECT ON CONTENT COMPREHENSION

Because speed reading requires the reader to suppress subvocalisation, you need to find a way to channel your concentration like a beam onto the text and zap up as much information as possible. The best way to improve a skill is by practicing, and if you do strategic practicing, your results may be even more successful. A practice method that is strategically aimed at improving comprehension while increasing reading speed at the same time is the stopwatch method. Let's look at an outline of how this method should be put into practice.

Allocate some time for yourself on a daily basis for the next few weeks. It can be anything from three to six weeks, depending on your ambitions. If you have ten to fifteen minutes to spare, that's perfect. You will be using this time every day to test and improve your speed reading and comprehension abilities by using the stopwatch method. The best way to stick to this new habit is by deciding on a specific time when you'll be doing your test each day and setting a reminder or alarm to help you remember. This will help the new activity to become a part of your daily routine. Now, let's look at how you'll be using the stopwatch approach to switch your brain into a new gear:

Your first task is to choose reading material that is suitable for developing speed reading comprehension. This means that the literature you decide to use shouldn't be super-complicated or too uncomplicated; a perfect example is a book like a paperback, whether it's fiction or nonfiction, that you have always wanted to read but never had the time to. It's also better if you don't know too much about the book's main idea beforehand, as this may influence your ability to assess your comprehension abilities when using the stopwatch method. Along with your reading material, you'll need to acquire a few paper clips and a stopwatch. You can use the stopwatch function on your smartphone, iPad, or your smartwatch. Everything seems to have a stopwatch and timer function these days.

Your "day 1" activities are going to be a once-off procedure and different from the rest of the days you'll be using your stopwatch method. Follow these guidelines meticulously:

1. On day one, you will need to set your timer for about seven to ten minutes. After starting your timer, read as much from your chosen source as you can, and when the time is up, use your paper clip to mark the last page you read and close the book. Before you can end your activity, you need to summarise the information you can remember from the book during your reading period. If you want to use more of your senses in this practice to improve the accelerated learning process, you can recite your summary out loud to yourself, which will then automatically involve your auditory and verbal skills. There's no standard or comprehension requirement at this stage, so after you've done this, you can put away your book until you get your next stopwatch reading reminder.
2. On your second day, you can open up your book at the paper clip and count how many pages you read the previous day. This will give you an indication of how many pages you need to read today, so you count the same number of pages forward in the book, add another one

page, and insert a paperclip. Use the same time setting you did the previous day and try to read all the new pages to the best of your ability during your seven to ten minutes. Now, you've read one more page than you did yesterday during the same time span. After the timer stops, follow the same pattern as the day before by summarising what you've read, and use a multisensory approach if it works for you.
3. Every subsequent day, you can follow the same procedure by adding one page and marking the place with a paperclip. After practicing this procedure for a week or two, you can start adding one page a few days apart instead of every day. This method is based on the idea that a reader needs to sacrifice comprehension if they want to increase their reading speed. However, if you as the reader force yourself into a situation where you set your own benchmark and then start increasing it by a small margin daily, which includes reading but also a subsequent summary of the content, you force your mind to develop strategies that assist you in attaining both goals.

The stopwatch method will also improve a skill prevalent in the most successful speed readers, which is "risk-taking". Risk-taking involves making educated guesses while speed reading by only absorbing specific parts of the text and developing the content with relevant knowledge that exists in your mind. This concept is a crucial element of successful reading, as well-planned reading involves the process of absorbing information from the text and linking it to what's in the mind.

We can also mention other comprehension techniques that are effective once you've reached your level of reading speed and are satisfied with your extent of comprehension, but let's look at them briefly, as they overlap with some of the retaining and basic speed-reading methods, as they are all so closely related.

The first aspect you're going to want to execute well is sizing up your task. This activity, if done mindfully, will reap many benefits later in the learning and speed reading process. So, assess what your aims are, or if you were appointed a task, what you need to do to accomplish it successfully. If you have a book in front of you, you need to get to the framework and main idea to set a basis for your comprehension abilities when you'll be speed reading.

Next, gather ideas that you have questions about. At this point, you will not know a lot about the text's content, so many of these questions may be at an instinctual level. However, they will help you identify the "gaps" and fill them in while you are reading at an increased pace. The trick is that if you are already aware of these questions and thoughts before or when you start your speed-reading practice, then experiencing that "aha" moment and linking relevant ideas during the speed-reading process doesn't need to be done from scratch, and each comprehension process can be completed quickly and effectively while pushing on with the reading.

A basic and useful tool that improves comprehension and speed reading simultaneously is to suppress subvocalisation. Pro tip: If you are not currently doing this while speed reading, try to fill your head with another source of sound, like music, to drown out your own subvocalisation. I suspect listening to Enya on a low volume may not be what is required here; you're going to need to push that second voice out of your head. Keep in mind that we speak much slower than we read, by a difference of about fifty to a hundred words, so when you constantly subvocalise everything you read, you will not be able to substantially increase your reading speed.

The method of blaring some rock or blues music into your ears is going to feel intrusive, because your brain will find it harder to subvocalise. However, because that's what we want to achieve, you just need to focus harder on reading and absorbing, as your brain will get used to the music and eventually block that out as well. Ultimately, you will end up with super-concentration abilities that will support your speed reading and boost your comprehension due to the decreased effect that subvocalisation has on your ability to read fast and understand quickly.

When we start reading as children, we learn to understand how syllables join together to become a word, and this is key to our comprehension of different words at that young age. However, as an older learner, this approach will slow you down, especially in speed reading endeavors. An adult has the ability to look at and absorb groups of words because their brains don't require them to recognise each syllable before they can recognise or understand a specific word. This is, as we mentioned earlier, called chunking.

Chunking is a beneficial tool for increasing your reading speed, but successful and strategic chunking can also boost comprehension. You can test your level of chunking comprehension by taking a text that you haven't read yet and grouping words together using a pen. Try not to read them at this point! You can start with small chunks and then move to larger chunks. After finishing your grouping process, you can set your mind into focus drive and look at the individual groups quickly before moving on. Did you understand what each chunk was telling you? If small chunks get too easy for you, divide your page into three or four parts and focus on the chunks to see if you can understand the content. As with the stopwatch method, a great idea is to repeat what you understand out loud to yourself after each exercise and then go back to the page to see if your interpretations are accurate. This time, your approach is just a bit more advanced, as you are reading groups of words at once.

And then, folks, it's important to remember to use that pointer! Whether it's your finger, a pen, or your computer's cursor, as long as it draws the eyes in the right direction and provides leadership and guidance for your mind, it can work. You can create speed reading magic with your pointer if your mind is ready and aligned to absorb and comprehend; it all comes down to understanding the technique and how the pointer assists your mind and eyes when reading.

Some things that you can keep in mind when using your pointer are to keep the pace steady and focused, remind yourself that the purpose of the pointer is so you don't go back to look at previous words (this will force you to concentrate), and to start at a reasonable speed when using this technique for the first time. Your brain will need to adjust to the technique and pull itself together when you use a pointer for the first time, but if you practice this technique consistently and avoid becoming impatient with the progress of your reading speed, the results will come streaming in. Pointing is a valuable tool for teaching your brain not to slack down but to comprehend as you read.

The next point is one that we haven't touched on a lot, but this tool is very useful for comprehension when it comes to speed reading. A side-goal you can set yourself every time you read is to develop and broaden your vocabulary. Reading material is the ideal source for this skill-development endeavor, as nobody wants to sit and read a dictionary every day. Having a broad vocabulary can help you in so many ways, and when it comes to comprehension in speed reading, it's like a magic potion.

Imagine you are speed reading a text, but there are one or two words that you don't understand, and they inhibit your ability to comprehend the entirety of what you are reading. Reading a lot helps a person to overcome this irritating issue by being able to understand new words and connect them contextually to other words that they, the reader, already know. Another advantage of having a broad vocabulary is understanding the subtle differences between synonyms and why a specific synonym is more suited to one context instead of another. This super-skill that comes from regularly acquiring new vocabulary can help a speed reader develop a very specific contextual view from text or literature in super-fast time, which also helps not only with basic comprehension, but also with using vocabulary knowledge to develop an even deeper sense of contextual comprehension.

The second-to-last technique is one that is focused on retention, but because retention and memory are so closely related, these overlapping ideas tend to come up again as the conversation and discussion continues. This technique is the recalling technique, and it is based on making a point of pausing and trying to recall as much as you can after reaching a specific point. If you are a beginner at speed reading, you may want to indicate in the text where you want to pause to implement this exercise, or if you are more advanced, you can also wait until the end of the page, chapter, or book to do the recalling exercise. Another great tip is, after you've identified when you want to do the recalling exercise, to take your pen and write down key words that you associate with the text. Keep your writing minimal and focus on the main idea while you practice the technique at every recollection point you set out for yourself.

The final technique is not only applicable to comprehension when it comes to speed reading, but also applies to any new activity or skill you aim to acquire. This final point, to me, is applicable to all new journeys we choose to take in life, but it is specifically reflected in the stopwatch method we discussed above when it comes to comprehension in speed reading. This technique is setting goals and targets, so you can plot your way toward achieving them. With speed reading, the best kinds of goals will be short-term goals because, as a beginner speed reader, you may not be able to estimate your own potential. So, don't place a ceiling over your abilities that you may have to destroy again or may not be able to reach because you don't know this side of yourself that well yet.

So, why is the stopwatch method such a great example of realistic goal-setting and progress-tracking? Firstly, you start off by estimating your own average abilities, so the goals you will set further down the line are less likely to be unattainable or unrealistic, except if purposefully calculated this way. So, this model of developing a technique shows you which components are required to reach attainable goals. For example, you can't estimate and set your goals based on someone else's reading speed or ability. For optimal comprehension development, estimate your average reading speed and comprehension abilities and slowly push yourself by setting attainable yet challenging goals. Don't "ceiling in" your expectations, but also don't set yourself up for disappointment. It's all about that balance in knowing, trusting, and pushing yourself forward.

RETAINING TIPS

Now that we've spent some time looking at practical methods that can boost comprehension, let's also look at some great retention tips. You can choose which ones you want to implement, or you can teach yourself to use all of them simultaneously. Again, they all fit into the broad idea of accelerated learning and its principles that are relevant to speed reading. All in all, there are five effective and mindful methods that will improve your retention abilities.

Inspectional Reading

By conducting your inspectional reading first, you will have some basics to work with when you move on to the rest of the techniques that we'll be discussing. So, inspectional reading is done for the purpose of getting what can be interpreted as the "pulse", the "main idea", or the "bird's-eye view" of the literature. The best way to achieve this is to look at a few single pages in the book, because you don't want to waste too much time. However, while doing this, you are looking for indications of what the underlying theme is. So, this is not even skimming, it's skimming's little cousin.

You can improve your chances of finding a good bird's-eye view while looking at fewer pages by being strategic regarding which page you choose to conduct your inspectional reading on. For example, if there is a foreword or a book description, you will likely find most of your information there, and if you want to be a tiny bit more thorough, you can look at the first page of each chapter and the first page of the conclusion. It also depends on what you have to work with. If it's an academic document, it hopefully has an abstract that is well-written, and this component should provide you with all the main details you need to move forward to the next technique. You can use this technique to find two main details for an effective start to your retention process: the main takeaway and the topic or main idea.

Be Curious

Never underestimate the power of curiosity. This mental superpower can help you retain at a significantly higher rate than if you had a lukewarm attitude toward your targeted text. Awakening that feeling of curiosity is like administering a top-quality primer to your brain that will ensure long-lasting and quality retention results. We, as humans, are intrinsically prone to do things that have a "rewarding effect" on our minds. The hormone that plays a central role in this "reward" process is dopamine, and it gives you that high after you've "received" your mental "reward". Dopamine is also the neurotransmitter that lights up when you get a "like" on social media, making you feel good about someone liking or appreciating your post. This can be used as a tool to retain more information faster if you know how to increase your dopamine production, because dopamine has shown to play a role in enhancing and connecting cells required for efficient learning.

Studies have indicated that when participants feel curious or intrigued, this process in the brain is activated and it is consequently linked to increased memory creation in the area of the hippocampus in the brain. So, do you feel like feeling a bit curious when you conduct your next speed reading excursion? Keep in mind that this needs to be genuine curiosity, because you can't fool your brain into producing dopamine by pretending to be intrigued. This means you need to use the knowledge you have about yourself, apply it to what you have to learn or read, and genuinely ask yourself which part of that text tickles your fancy.

One way of doing this is by thinking of "curiosity gap" questions before you start your reading process. A "curiosity gap" exists when there is an empty space or vacuum in an idea that you want to know more about; for example, something that is not explicitly expressed or explained. Aim to identify these gaps and use them to fuel your curiosity when you want to read fast and retain as much as possible.

Don't forget to be curious about your vocabulary too. It might seem counterproductive, but if you are speed reading and come across words you don't know the meaning of, go back once you have finished your set time and look them up. Use a thesaurus to learn even more words. The sooner you can expand your vocabulary, the easier speed reading becomes.

Give It Meaning

One way to improve retention and to feel like you're not wasting your time is to find your own personal angle that gives meaning to the information you are reading and why you are reading it. For example, ask yourself some questions about the content and your intentions like, "Why do I want to read this?" Or "How is this going to improve my life and how will I benefit personally?" Additionally, you can also go down the aisle of, "What does this mean to me?" and, "Does it have any meaning?" Another interesting assessment you can conduct in terms of finding your angle is to figure out who the intended audience is, if you are part of this audience, and why. Because relevance awakens emotion within us, you can use this to your advantage and as a retention tool when you need to read fast and efficiently. All that is required are questions that pre-program your mind and a subsequent change in mindset.

Organising and Structuring

Organising and structuring refers to your personal take on arranging things in a way that will help you to absorb and retain at your best. This can include a variety of techniques; however, if your organisational and structuring methods are based on using the visual part of your brain, like with a mind map, you will get the most from it. This is because your brain will then automatically organise information in whichever way you perceive it and its connections to be most relevant and intelligible.

Readers tend to want to understand content in the structure that the author or editor placed it in from their perspective. However, if a reader wants to step up the retention phase a notch, they can detach themselves from the author or editor's writing structure and connect the dots differently. The first thing you would want to do is scan through the text or literature and identify the structure used by the author. Does this structure resonate with you inherently? If so, that's a bonus and you don't have to make many changes to your mind-mapping. However, if there is a structure that will be more suited to your personal approach to learning and reading, you can give yourself a hand by starting to identify main concepts, use them to divide the entire text into sizable chunks that have personal relevance, and to leave space for your own thoughts and interpretations.

A Note Never Hurt Anyone

One would never think that speed reading could be connected to notetaking, but there are so many contributing factors that include different types of literature and texts that are suitable for speed reading and benefits of notetaking. This is also directly linked to what the speed reader wants to achieve with the speed-reading process, so a recording or note-taking process is definitely relevant when the aim is to retain what you've read. That doesn't mean it has to be boring or that it should remind you of Mrs. Schnickler from middle school who used to force you to copy all her notes from the blackboard. This is your approach and your space, and that's what's going to make you successful in the end.

Let's start by looking at what we want to do to our brains when we record or take notes, because that's the important part. When we use a recording method, we require it to forge new pathways in the brain. Therefore, writing sentence after sentence is not going to help if there is no meaning or context connected to it. The way you do it is up to you; for example, if you prefer highlighting because the bright colours draw your eye back to previous key phrases or information, then do that. Do whatever works best for you.

However, be sure to record with meaning. Focus on small chunks at a time, and make sure that you understand why you've recorded the information and how it fits into what you are busy reading. Then, when your eye flits back to these notes or highlighted portions, your brain will be able to make instant connections with information you are reading that may be a few pages or paragraphs on. This crossover connection technique that recording and note-taking warrants rocket-fuels the process from connecting ideas to comprehension and, ultimately, retention.

PRACTICE MAKES PERFECT

Every technique and method discussed so far points to the fact that if you want to acquire the speed-reading superpower, you need to practice. In the end, there are many components that can help you to become a pro speed reader, but it starts by identifying your abilities and intelligence type.

I love horse riding, as does my mom. When I was a kid, my mom would always tell me that to ride well depends more on how much work you put in than how much talent you have. Almost like the 20/80 rule. At least, that's the ratio you need to base your efforts on if you want to be successful at something. That's not what I wanted to hear, because I wanted to do everything perfectly the first time, but I only realised the truth and value in what she said when I got older. Nobody is going to reach the same top speed while also having the same level of comprehension, so you have to work with your body. In the next chapter, we're going to look at how you can integrate classic accelerated learning ideas and techniques so that you don't just use speed reading when you are in a rush, but rather make a habit out of it and improve every time you enter your learning space.

5

INTEGRATING IDEAS

We now know substantially more about accelerated learning and speed reading. Both can help you reach a level of potential you've only dreamed of when it comes to learning, potential, and self-improvement. Accelerated learning has a rich history of research and it is all about a holistic approach to learning that accommodates all types of minds and personalities. We can even take it a step further by looking at some accelerated learning techniques that you, as a self-learner, can use to improve the space you place yourself in when you decide to learn and use techniques like speed reading.

We shouldn't underestimate the importance of the learning environment and the effect it has on us from a multisensory perspective. Our disregard or dismissive attitude towards this aspect may come from time spent in a traditional educational environment where these aspects were not deemed important or incorporated, so making them important can require a mind-shift and the development of a fresh perspective.

TRY INTEGRATING THESE ACCELERATED LEARNING TECHNIQUES

Because learning can either be exciting or terrifying, it's always prudent to use all the tools you have at your disposal to create your optimal learning environment and develop compatible and personalised methods. Accelerated learning has repeatedly been lauded as a successful productive process, and even though it may be most beneficial when applied in a classroom from a young age, there are just as many benefits for adult self-learners, as they already possess knowledge that young children still need to discover about themselves. There is a myriad of online tests and apps that can help you to discover your basic strengths and aptitudes, which is the starting block. After that, the sky's the limit! Consider these basic methods, some of which I have previously mentioned but not discussed in detail, as auxiliary tools for creating a speed reading and accelerated learning utopia.

Multisensory Learning

Multisensory learning means that you are going to identify your sensory strengths, but still use the most beneficial gains from the other senses. So, we've got our visual, aural, verbal, and physical traits. We now know that visual learners become accustomed to speed reading easily because visual capabilities are the main requirement. However, while speed reading focuses on visual capabilities, accelerated learning focuses on activating as many parts of the brain as possible according to the strengths of the learner. If you are a strong visual learner, how will you incorporate a kinesthetic approach to your speed-reading process? Or should you first ask yourself if incorporating this component will improve your speed-reading technique? Maybe sitting on a comfy chair or under a cozy blanket when it's cold can elevate your comfort level and help you to concentrate. The first thing I thought about when I considered a kinesthetic component was that I had to speed read while standing in tree pose because I have to use my body. However, feeling and being sensitive to textures is also a kinesthetic attribute and strength.

Mind-Mapping

Mind-mapping, which we mentioned earlier when discussing how to retain information, is defined by a central idea that the learner visually represents information for themselves by placing it in hierarchies that make the most sense to them. The central idea is used to develop the different branches and related topics, which helps the reader to create a large mental image of a text or piece of literature and how all its components fit together.

This method is not a new concept in any way or form, but it has recently been re-introduced by an individual named Tony Buzan. The benefits of mind-mapping in speed reading are that it can help you to identify and establish connections between multiple components in the text, and by placing them in a hierarchical structure in your mind, you can help yourself understand how they fit together and retain this information for longer. Think groups and subgroups. If you're a visual learner, you can create a vivid mind map with lots of shapes and detail. If you're a logical learner, you may be more comfortable with a mind map that looks like a neatly constructed diagram. If you are auditory, you can associate sounds or music with different components to incorporate your own learning dominance with this visually-oriented tool.

Stay in That Relaxed Space

Although relaxing to the point where you completely switch off your mind will not help you much if you want to create the ultimate speed reading or learning space, relaxing is a crucial component of efficient learning. Therefore, concentration or focus should not be associated with stress. Because concentration requires a lot of energy, one can become exhausted and need to step away from the learning space. The key here is to maintain a relaxed and calm attitude, as stress may alienate you from your previous, positive learning space. If you are tired or anxious, this is also a sign that you need to give your mind a break, in order to maintain a healthy relationship with your learning space. Relaxing in today's frantic environment is an ability that requires mastering on its own.

You can help yourself relax while studying by taking brief breaks where you do breathing exercises, take a power nap, or you can try meditating to recenter your mind. The most important thing to remember is that your performance will be significantly better if you are calm and relaxed, so if you feel that you need to realign, take the steps that work for you to get you back into that relaxed space.

Create a Focused Space

The purpose of this focused space is to provide comfort and support relaxation on all sensory levels while accentuating your main learning style. There's a lot you can do to create and customise your focused space, but the first thing we should think about is the state you should be in when you enter this space. Before you create your focused space, promise yourself that you will never enter this space without being prepared to focus on improvement and excellence. Every positive entry into this space will reinforce future successes.

Let's start with a space that is easily accessible and that you will also find comfortable to focus in. Could this space be in your bedroom, or maybe outside on the veranda? Alternatively, you may have a dedicated working space like a study, where you do most of your reading. After you've identified this space, you can start adding, removing, or enhancing components that affect your ability to focus. Let's start with the lighting in the room. Is there sufficient light? Is the light too bright or do you perhaps need more light?

The best light is natural light, but nature doesn't follow our learning schedules, so the next-best thing is to acquire a light source that provides quality lighting that will, for example, not put strain on your eyes.

Moving on from the light, how does the colour of the environment affect you? They say that colours have different effects on one's mood, but I think an individual's personal perspective is also important here. For example, red and orange are supposed to fuel anger, agitation, and irritation, but many people love these colours and feel happy and comfortable being surrounded by red or orange walls. Maybe you like your neutrals and your walls are cream, beige, or off-white. You can even thrive if surrounded by a spectrum of colour; that is the beauty of this discussion and what you can take away from it. If you are unsure and you want to base your choice on research, the best colors to surround yourself with are blue or green, due to their calming effects.

Then, some individuals are very sensitive to sound, and while some prefer to listen to some sort of music to help them focus, there are those who prefer complete silence. In the past, students were encouraged to listen to Baroque music like works from Bach and Scarlatti, but these days, you can download countless auditory study aids, from white noise apps to the sound of wind and rain and eccentric harmonisations.

I remember when, in high school, I had a maths lesson in a classroom with a fluorescent light that made a terrible humming sound. This sound irritated me so much that I would have preferred having the class in a darker room or even to have done self-study, as the sound still buzzed in my head long after math was over and I was sitting in another classroom trying to focus. This is an example of a component in your study space that appears to provide a benefit but that actually prevents you from focusing. Do you have a noisy light? If you're not an auditory learner, it may not even bother you in the end, so we need to look at all of these details hypothetically. However, I think it's best to include only beneficial sounds into a focused learning space—ones that promote focus—even if you are not aware of them all the time. Let's leave a detailed discussion of auditory aids for the last section below:

Incorporate Music

The variety of study sounds or music that are currently accessible to all of us must be the most enjoyable part of the process to experiment with for me. I grew up with the advice that one should listen to Bach, but I never really knew why. Today, there are also other kinds of music and even sounds that are deemed beneficial for improving your concentration and relaxing your mind. Think about running on a treadmill for thirty minutes while listening to some upbeat music versus running on the same treadmill for the same amount of time in silence. Do you think running while listening to some nice beats in your ears will let the time pass by a little faster while you're pushing your body? You may even run a little faster and have a more successful workout. Consider this and then compare your thoughts to running on the treadmill with no music. How long do you think you will last if you don't enjoy listening to your own fatigued breathing? This really makes you think of how music helps people to push themselves when they are exercising. So, do you think that this potent effect can also be relevant to one's ability to concentrate while reading or learning?

The integration of music into learning spaces is not only a hot topic in the educational sector, but seasoned entrepreneurs and businessmen have also discovered the benefits of using sound to alter and relax the mind and boost concentration. Music from the Baroque and Classical eras is still lauded for its ability to aid learning and concentration. This method has previously been coined the "Mozart Effect," and it is based on studies that indicate classical music can improve an individual's ability to solve puzzles of a spatial nature and to manipulate shapes. One of the reasons classical music is so effective may be because it does not contain any lyrics, so has no distracting words that the listener would have to process on top of the information they are trying to absorb. Top composers to choose from include Bach, Mozart, Vivaldi, and Beethoven. Another approach is using sounds from nature to create a calm atmosphere. I assume that there is already a consensus not to include sounds of treacherous thunder, hurricanes, earthquakes, or any recent typhoons in this category. Sounds like soft rainfall, waves gently crashing on a shore, or water flowing down a stream also have the potential to improve cognitive function and these sounds can be easily downloaded or streamed from an app or computer browser. Gentle nature sounds have been found to also have a restorative effect on individuals' cognitive function apart from improving focus.

Another stimulating option that has been tried and tested is film scores. These scores are often dramatic and, if listened on their own without the movie, can be put in an entirely different context. Essentially, the dramatic and grand nature of film scores can give the listener a feeling of empowerment whilst relaxing and opening up the mind. Two scores that come recommended are the ones from "The Bourne Identity" and "Cloud Atlas". These sources of music are also easy to find, so you can build your own collection specifically for when you need to focus.

An option that is actually very similar to film scores is video game music. Because so many games are based on a plot and storyline, these games have the same type of music as films. The nature of the music will also most likely be ambitious and energetic, which will resonate well with a learner that needs inspiration. One of the aims of video game music is to help keep the player engaged, so you will definitely experience a cognitive boost if it falls within your musical preference. You can start by looking at the music from games like Assassin's Creed, Final Fantasy, and Skyrim.

The next theory I want to add for your consideration is not based on the music itself, but specifically the tempo of the music. Researchers say that for music to be cognitively stimulating, the tempo must be between fifty and eighty beats per minute. If you listen to music within this beat range, your brain will automatically switch to an alpha state, which means that you are more receptive than when you are in your normal beta state Alpha state describes the brain when we are awake and in a state of heightened alertness. This is definitely interesting to know, and it doesn't necessarily exclude all the options we discussed above. It does, however, typically include pop music from artists like Adele, Justin Timberlake, and Bruno Mars.

Now that we've gone through so many options, are there any options left? If none of these options work for you, the best thing to do is to listen to your favourite music. Yes, it can also be that easy. If your favourite music has not been mentioned in the discussion above, then you can still use the music you like if it has a positive effect on your cognitive functioning. However, if the music is an emotional trigger more than a cognitive booster, it's not going to have the desired effect. It's your call.

6

MAINTAIN YOUR BRAIN

We've taken in a lot so far; some things even more than once but from different perspectives. That's the nature of holistic and multifaceted methods: one concept can be used and applied more than one way, and if beneficial, it should be. However, whichever methods you are using, the brain should be kept running like a well-oiled machine to maintain high learning and reading potential, and our hectic lifestyles don't always allow us to keep up with the maintenance. This chapter will focus on providing basic details about cognitive health for a healthy brain, while also emphasising that, if you want to make a lifestyle change or start taking vitamins or supplements, the best way to ensure that it's right for you is to visit your physician. Going for regular checkups can help your doctor identify any issues before they become life-altering problems. On the other side, this chapter will also be able to provide you with some insight about what your brain needs to be healthy, what your body needs to be healthy, and what your soul needs to be healthy.

The brain is an integral part of the human body, so if your body experiences health issues, it can also affect your cognitive functioning acutely, or in more serious cases, chronically. Think about when you come down with the common cold. Not only do you cough and sneeze, but you also feel tired and cranky because your body needs to use energy to recover. You will only regain your mental clarity when the cold is cleared up and you've allowed your body to recover and rest. Let's start off by looking at what constitutes a healthy brain and how to develop and maintain one for reaching your full potential.

A HEALTHY BRAIN FOR UNLOCKING YOUR FULL POTENTIAL

The healthiest brain is one with a healthy and positive attitude. But what does this mean? Using "attitude" is barely a scientific way to look at brain function; however, it is one of the telltale characteristics of a healthy mind.

Always being reminded of staying positive doesn't mean that you are not allowed to be exhausted, angry, frustrated, or sad; it's the way you deal with these situations that indicate how healthy you are. And a desire to be healthy should also be regarded as a healthy thought process. These emotive responses and experiences are integrally linked with our brain's physical health and whether there are any imbalances or deficiencies. Because of our lifestyles, the types of food available, the ridiculously limited amount of time we have to spend on our health and self-care, and the cost of living, being healthy has become an art in itself. Being healthy today requires careful planning, potential professional input, and enthusiastic execution.

Our brains all look the same except for the fact that they may ever-so-slightly vary in size and shape, but they are also very different. They are diverse, they have different strengths, and they may have different nutritional needs. Some of us, most likely, have developed needs due to factors from our childhood that can include nutrition or psychological factors, while some may have an existing medical condition that requires treatment. Apart from all of these factors, there are nutritional components that all of us can look at and consider in order to improve and maintain optimal brain health. Let's look at some ways, this time from a general point of view, that we can feed and nourish the brain on a nutritional level.

DEVELOP A SUPER BRAIN

To maintain a healthy mind physiologically and live a quality life, you can look at a few nutritional additions that specifically help the nerve centers in your brain to improve and maintain their functioning. The older generation (at least the ones that I know) are known for complaining about how they were forced to swallow a teaspoon of cod liver oil every day as children. I wonder if they know how lucky they are. That fishy taste is known to linger in your mouth, hover on your breath, and stick to the hand that touched the darned bottle, but if you know what's hidden in this repulsive and oily substance, you may consider taking a double dose.

. . .

Meet the Omegas

Most of us are familiar with three types of omegas: Omega-3, Omega-6, and omega-9. All three are known as essential fatty-acids, and while these sources are important for bodily functioning, our bodies cannot produce all of these fatty acids on their own. Omega-3 fatty acids are one of the most important supporters of brain and cognitive health. Our brains use omega-3 fatty acids to maintain and create new neural connections, which enables us to process information every day and to use our body in the most functional way possible. The brain also uses omega-3 fatty acids as a form of fuel that enables it to create the energy the body needs to function normally. These essential fatty acids are also extremely important for the healthy development of an unborn baby, and pregnant women are encouraged to take omega-3 supplements during their pregnancy to reduce any risks of the child having visual, behavioural, learning, or attention problems after birth.

The most important omega-3s the body and the brain need are long-chain fatty acids called EPAs and DHAs. This is because the brain consists of 60% fat, and these fats are classified as healthy, essential fats. DHA, which is the most common fatty acid found in the human brain, is mainly responsible for creating connective activity in the brain and the retina, which is located in the eye. This means that DHA is largely responsible for lighting up our eyeballs and subsequently processing what they see, which is a pretty important job for a long-chain fatty acid that cannot be generated by the body itself. On the other hand, EPA is not as common in the human body, specifically the brain, but it is mainly responsible for nerve cell production and managing healthy responses to inflammation that is specifically related to your joints and circulation, among others.

Another extremely relevant reason to consider keeping your omega-3 levels healthy is this fatty acid's therapeutic effect on anxiety and depression. These conditions can greatly affect one's ability to concentrate and learn, and omega-3 fatty acids have a distinct effect on the production of the stress hormone called cortisol. EPA, specifically, has a proven effect on reducing performance anxiety, like the type of stress you would experience before an exam or test. Of course, if you are experiencing any type of symptoms related to anxiety or depression, it's important to consult your physician as soon as possible.

Omega-3 fatty acids are found in different edible sources, which include walnuts, cold-water fish, olive oil, and even garlic. However, the human body finds it difficult to convert the EPAs and DHAs it needs from plant-based omega-3 sources, so the best source for these fatty acids is fish oil or, if required, a concentrated form of fish oil that contains the EPA and DHA ratios you need.

To calculate whether an individual may have an omega-3 deficiency and as an indication of general health, there is a measuring system called the Omega-3 Index. The Omega-3 Index shows you what your omega-3 levels are, which can help you estimate if you should eat more omega-3-rich foods or take a supplement. Measurements in the United States have indicated that the average American's Omega 3 Index level is well below the required index value. If you have an index value of eight percent or more, you are considered to have adequate omega-3 levels or "omega-3 status." If you can be classified as an "average American," you may have an average index of just over five, which is well below the recommended index level of eight.

Apart from omega-3 fatty acids, the body also requires omega-6 fatty acids, as they are also not generated by the body. However, omega-6 fatty acids are so prevalent in foods we eat regularly in a modern diet that an omega-6 supplement may not be required. You can find omega-6 fatty acids in a lot of fast food like fries, onion rings, and fried chicken due to their presence in different vegetable oils, including canola and sunflower oil. Other commonly consumed foods include cereals, eggs, dairy products, and even baked goods like bread and muffins.

The reason this is important is because a balanced ratio between omega-3 fatty acids and omega-6 fatty acids is important to get the ultimate health benefits. Omega-6 fatty acids are important for optimal organ functioning, but their intake needs to be in balance with omega-3 and -9 fatty acids. Omega-9 fatty acids can luckily be generated by the body, so we are not as dependent on the consumption of specific foods for omega-9-related benefits.

The final part of omegas that needs attention and consideration is the ideal ratio and its subsequent intake requirements. What do we need to know about our omega intake requirements? Firstly, there is one essential fatty acid in omega-6 and one essential fatty acid in omega-3, known as the two "parent" fatty acids that the body requires through nutritional intake. They are known as alpha-linolenic acid (ALA) in omega-3 and linolenic acid (LA) in omega-6. Although a research-based ratio has not been established yet, it is recommended that we focus on omega-3 fatty acid supplements to even out the ratio with omega-6 fatty acids that are already so prevalent in our diet. Omega-3 is also essential because EPA and DHA cannot be produced in the body and, as seen above both of them, especially EPA, have a lot of health benefits for learners and individuals who are focused on mental wellbeing. Hopefully, this part of the book wasn't as bad as swallowing a big tablespoon of cod liver oil.

The Vitamin B Family

The vitamin B family always welcomes everyone with open arms. They are often neglected in our diets, but they are eager helpers in many a health department. There are quite a few members in the vitamin B family, so we're going to focus on those that help you improve that cognitive superpowers and at the foods that can help you achieve this.

Increasing your vitamin B intake does not mean you have to take a myriad of supplements: you can achieve this by following a vitamin B-rich diet or eating vitamin B-rich foods. Let's introduce the fam. There are eight B-vitamins, namely vitamin B1 (Thiamine), B2 (Riboflavin), B3 (Niacin), B5 (pantothenic acid), B6 (Biotin), B9 (Folate), and B12. All the vitamin Bs are plant-based except for B12, which is found in animal-based foods like dairy, fish, and eggs. Now, because your brain is always up to something, it is regarded as the most active organ in the body, metabolically speaking. And each member of the vitamin B family has a different task to perform when it comes to the transportation of other vitamins from the bloodstream into the brain.

When it comes to brain power and performance, members B6, B12, and B9 or Folate are associated with increased memory, problem-solving, the formation of words and sentences. I know, we don't want to formulate them, we want to read them at an increased speed, but your B-family has such a multi-functional role in overall brain health that it's hard to imagine a high level of cognitive functioning without them.

Another question that curious individuals often ask about the vitamin B-family is whether it is possible to get your recommended daily amount (RDA) from your diet or if one should take a supplement. Because there are so many different members in the vitamin B family, it is possible to develop a deficiency of one of them or a condition that is related to such a deficiency or that causes a deficiency. If you suspect that you are deficient, the best option is to visit your physician so the proper tests can be conducted for a diagnosis and subsequent treatment. If you are healthy and suspect that you don't have any deficiencies, a diet that contains foods rich in vitamin Bs is a great option.

Here are a variety of foods that contain high amounts of vitamin B: Beef liver, vitamin B12-enriched cereal, tuna fish, and milk are examples of sources that contain vitamin B12. Then, chickpeas, salmon, spinach, and raisins contain vitamin B6, while Brussel sprouts, broccoli, and medium-grain rice all contain folic acid. These are by no means all of your options and, if you like beef liver, it is actually a good source of all three types of vitamin B!

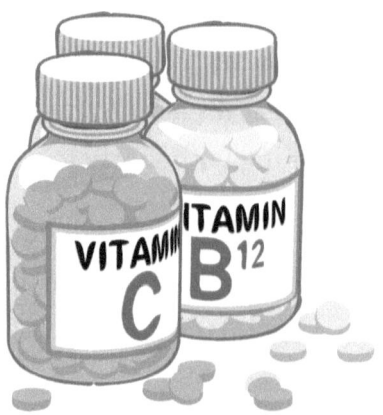

Superfoods

Superfoods is actually a postmodern buzzword that, for some reason, always hid away in the shelves of those health shops you never considered visiting. As this trend emerged and became mainstream in the past few decades, people began to discover the health benefits of everything green, and many of them from under the sea. I always thought health shops only sold mounds of green tea and weird root vegetables, but now I know that green is the most diverse colour in the world of superfoods and super health. If you want to go green, here are three options that can help boost your brain. Just remember to still eat your veggies!

The first superfood to consider is spirulina. Spirulina is a type of blue-green algae that lives in fresh or saltwater and is thought to have been used by the ancient Aztecs quite some time ago. After the Aztecs disappeared, the benefits of spirulina lay quiet for millennia, until NASA came to the rescue by claiming that this organism can be grown in outer space, thereby recultivating curiosity for this strange green substance. Spirulina has an extremely high level of several nutrients, including copper, vitamin B1, B2, and B3, and iron. Other notable nutrients include potassium, manganese, and magnesium, and most other nutrients are also included. The reasons you would want to ask your doctor about spirulina include its powerful inflammatory and antioxidant properties, its ability to improve endurance, its positive effect on cholesterol and blood pressure, and its preventive effect against conditions like anemia. Spirulina is available in a powder and tablet form and the recommended daily dosage is one tablespoon of seven grams. If you are looking for a basis on which you can build better physical and mental health, this is a great first option.

The second superfood that is so deliciously green is moringa. This plant is also known as *Moringa oleifera*, and it is consumed in a powder form. The powder comes from the pods and leaves of this tree, which is common in Africa, South America, and Asia. This superfood is high in calcium, potassium, and iron. Moringa powder is regarded as a superfood as it can help with common health issues related to heart problems, cholesterol, and diabetes. Apart from this, it provides an incredibly wide variety of nutrients that make it easier to sustain a healthy lifestyle. Because moringa is consumed in a very similar way to spirulina, it is easy to mix the powder in a drink or smoothie to get your daily nutrient boost.

The final superfood is the most popular one due to its high nutrient level and non-toxic stimulant properties. Yes, I'm talking about matcha. This hidden Japanese gem has made quite a grand entrance in the world of superfoods and is consumed by every second model walking the Versace catwalk; whether it's a latte, smoothie, or a tea (I have yet to see a scientific genius walk the streets with a matcha latte, though, but I think they prefer to stay indoors).

Let's take a closer look at this bright-green miracle. The first benefit that awards matcha rave reviews is the sustainable energy high it provides without the coffee-related anxiety. This high has been described as more of a "calm" high than the frantic high associated with copious amounts of coffee. Matcha is not caffeine-free, but because of the type of energy you experience after consuming matcha, it is considered a healthier and cleaner stimulant. It is also the caffeine combined with L-theanine in matcha that makes it so incredibly effective for times when you need to focus. L-theanine has the same effect on the brain as the classical music we discussed as part of our integration strategy; it activates alpha waves in the brain, which promotes relaxation and creates a sensation of mental clarity. This state enables you to absorb more and thus learn more as you are in a relaxed state of mental focus. Imagine what your brain might do when you drink matcha while listening to Beethoven's Moonlight Sonata.

The other reasons you may want to consider matcha are that it has immune-boosting properties, improves cognitive function, has high levels of antioxidants, and elevates the metabolism. This option seems to be an all-in-one, so keep it in mind when looking for a pick-me-up.

These are not the only superfoods out there. Even though they have more in common than the colour green, some may have more benefits than others, especially the benefits your body needs. Just remember to not develop the "now I don't have to eat my veggies" mentality, as a balanced diet is key.

Moving Those Limbs

I don't know about you, but if you are not really into fitness these days, all the terminology and concepts can be a bit intimidating. It appears that a lot of scientific research has gone into biokinetics and fitness, and consequently, normies like me are left with concepts and acronyms we don't understand. We can go through them to clarify what they mean, but I think what's important to know is that to be healthy, and to maintain a healthy brain, one doesn't need to do intense exercise every day for an hour. Not even every second day. Let's clarify this by looking at HIIT, LISS, and NEAT.

HIIT is also known as high intensity interval training, and you need to be relatively fit and strong to power through a HIIT workout. The duration is shorter, but the intensity is very high, and you can expect to maintain a high average heart rate during a HIIT workout. These types of workouts are for individuals who focus on fitness and maintain a fitness regime along with a fitness goal. I can say this because I don't think anybody would go through all that huffing and puffing if there wasn't a bigger picture keeping them glued to their goal.

LISS, on the other hand, is known as low intensity steady state training. The main difference between HIIT and LISS is that LISS is done at a considerably lower intensity and for a longer duration. If you are very concerned about burning fat, then LISS may not be your best bet. These two types of cardiovascular training are commonly used in conjunction with strength training for slimming and sculpting purposes.

However, if you are not particularly interested in fitness or body-sculpting, then relying on NEAT can help you to maintain a healthy body and mind if you consciously make an effort to maintain a respectable or health-boosting level. NEAT stands for non-exercise activity thermogenesis. NEAT involves all your activities that are not related to working out, eating, or sleeping. By giving your NEAT a little push, you don't have to go to the gym or do laborious crunches every other day. That is, if fitness is not one of your life pursuits.

A few ways you can push your NEAT up a notch is by making sure you meet a specific step count every day, spending more time standing, being active when taking breaks from work (for example by taking a walk), and doing tasks like cleaning and gardening yourself. Of course, carrying your smartphone with you or wearing a smartwatch like a Fitbit or an Apple Watch can help you keep track of your activities and set goals for yourself. They say that you should aim for ten thousand steps a day. I've even heard people say that, in order to reach this, they would purposefully make themselves take detours instead of walking straight toward whatever they want to clean or close or open. It's like circling the couch ten times before going to make your afternoon (matcha) tea. However, it seems to improve people's wellbeing, and that's why they keep doing it.

THE S-WORD

Yes, the S-word. We need to talk about this before we go. Stress can build you up or break you down, and healthy coping mechanisms are essential to performing any other task in your life with proficiency.

For example, we've discussed all of these superfoods and essential vitamins and fatty acids, so now you know that omega-3 can help you minimize your body's cortisol production, which is the stress hormone. However, even though omega-3 helps in this department, you still need to be mindful about how much stress you expose yourself to. The Stoic philosophers, who lived more than two thousand years ago, were very adamant about the fact that they would only stress about matters they were able to change. If it's a matter that they could not control or change, they did not see the purpose or usefulness of stressing about it, as it would only cause them unnecessary harm.

This, to me, is almost impossible, and I wonder if they were actually able to achieve this. However, even though Stoicism is relatively unpopular because it is deemed emotionless and cold, this take from them is one we should consider because of its self-preservation attribute. As modern individuals, we worry about absolutely everything. Take the weather for example: we'll most likely stress about whether the rain is going to ruin our outing to the theme park or the golf course tomorrow. If you think about it, we are actually worrying about something that is, ultimately, supposed to relax us. The purpose of playing golf and visiting the theme park is to relax and have fun, so why would you stress about it in any shape or form? The Stoics would have been completely bewildered at this logic, as the weather is the last thing we should be concerned about; it is completely out of our control. So, from their perspective, if it rains, we stay at home and make pizza. If the sun shines, we go on our outing as planned. Simple as that!

This is an example of how you can discern between what is worthy of stress and what is not. However, if the reason for stressing is validated, then coping with it mindfully is the most important task at hand. So, what if you are in a situation that warrants and deserves stress? For example, what if it's the night before a big test or fifteen minutes before you have to deliver a speech in front of the Save The Mountains committee, but you are not prepared? The Stoics would say, "HA! You should've prepared!" Well, that's why you now know how to chunk, skim, and minimize your subvocalisation, on top of creating your ideal space for focus and concentration. If these still need some practice, it is also important to remember (and this is hard) that stress and its symptoms will only exacerbate whatever you are trying to achieve. Take a moment to align your thoughts and to remind yourself what's worth focusing on. Rationalise the ineffectiveness of stress and how, after this is all over, you will thank yourself for conquering stress. You can do all of this and more in your ideal space where you can achieve clarity of mind and relax with the purpose of absorbing and learning.

CONCLUSION

When you look back at all the information you went through in this book, what would be the most important and profound concept you can take away? Alternatively, do you think you can personalise or add some hacks of your own to this collection of ideas aimed at improving your learning skills and reading ability? Either way, you improved your cognitive functioning by reaching, processing, comprehending, and retaining the main ideas. If you want to start pursuing accelerated learning or speed reading, that's the best way to get into it.

Looking back at all the information in *The Art of Accelerated Learning*, the most profound ideas that stood out to me are how educators and psychoanalysis identified the need to diversify the approach to education and the educational environment by studying the nature of intelligence and how it manifests in different ways. The traditional methods really did focus on one intelligence type, one way of thinking, and encouraged uniformity among students. When looking back at all that traditional educational methods stand for, it seems so out of place in our postmodern and diverse approach to life overall.

It's actually amazing to suddenly realise how we differ when it comes to our learning styles, and how people still went through the traditional system and pushed through, irrespective of the fact that it was ill-accommodating. People are resilient and strong, and they deserve to know their potential and be granted the opportunity to develop it to the fullest. There are so many tips and tricks that everyone can take from the concept of accelerated learning, even if we are not focused learners. This must be due to its extensive development and the research dedicated to its successful implementation. We, as humans, are perpetual learners, and being cognizant of this fact can help us understand our environment, our potential, and our future success.

Speed reading seems to be more of a self-learning experience than a recipe-type skill-learning process. It's come forth so many times that one needs to take a step back, be non-judgmental, and use patience in order to achieve the optimal results. The speed reading learner should also bear in mind that it is not about reaching the maximum reading speed, but more about increasing the reading speed to a realistic and comfortable level. Additionally, along with this increase, the other component of speed reading that is crucial is developing a heightened state of comprehension and retention with the reading process. There are individuals who can read at an incomprehensible speed, but this can be due to their specific aptitude and intelligence type or learning style.

Because we have the background of accelerated learning, we also know that you can't set goals based on other people's performance, because of our differences in intelligence types and learning styles. There is, however, a seemingly bottomless pit of resources and tools one can use to become the best speed reader in one's own right. The trick is to survey the numbers and statistics, apply your individual role-players, and to push with patience. Whatever you want to achieve with speed reading, the sky's the limit. The reason why speed reading is so common among high-level executives and businessmen is because these individuals possibly have one thing in common: they don't underestimate themselves.

Finally, looking at all the other resources at our disposal for self-improvement and optimal health, the first and best step would be to make a habit out of getting your regular checkups. Feeling tired or irritated all the time, for example, is not natural, so you can start by looking at whether you're getting all your nutrients in your diet and if you are getting enough sleep. You need a healthy body to carry a healthy mind, and vice versa, so it's crucial for you to be in tune with and understanding of your body's needs. The vitamin B family is always there to help, and now you know where to find them. Remember about your omegas and to consume omega-3-rich foods. And, finally, consider adding a superfood, not as a replacement for a healthy diet, but to boost your overall health and wellbeing.

One thing I want you to take away from this book is the concept of diversity—the idea that even though there were so many concepts, ideas, and methods mentioned and discussed in this book, you only need to take those into account that you identify with and that will help you succeed. Keep in mind that it is beneficial to be aware of the others, because you can learn from everything you expose yourself to. However, this book and everything it discusses should be regarded as a joyous celebration of all intelligence types and their limitless potential.

I would love to hear all of your experiences and successes, what has worked for you and how learning has become more enjoyable and effective. Leaving a quick Amazon review is a great way to help others improve their learning. Good Luck!

Thank you for reading my book The Art of Accelerated Learning. If you have enjoyed reading it perhaps you would like to leave a star rating and a review for me? It really helps support writers like myself create more books.

Please scan this QR code with your phones camera and you will be re-directed to the Amazon review page.

Thank you so much. Selena Watts

REFERENCES

8 Exercises to Improve Your Reading Speed and Comprehension. (2020). https://theutopianlife.com/2017/05/07/8-exercises-to-improve-your-reading-speed-and-comprehension/

21 Health Benefits of Matcha Green Tea. Tenzo Matcha. (2020). https://tenzotea.co/pages/21-health-benefits-matcha-green-tea.

Accelerated Learning - The Peak Performance Center. (2020). https://thepeakperformancecenter.com/educational-learning/learning/theories/accelerated-learning/

Accelerated Learning - Creative Wealth International. (2020). https://www.creativewealthintl.org/

accelerated- learning.php#:~:text=History%20of%20Accelerated %20Learning%3A&text

Accelerated Learning Principles. (2009). https://www.learningdoorway.com/ accelerated-learning-principles.html

Bedosky, L., & Kennedy, K. (2019). The Science-Backed Health Benefits of Moringa Powder (M. Oleifera) | Everyday Health. EverydayHealth.com.https://www.everydayhealth.com/ diet-nutrition/diet/science-backed-health- benefits-moringa-powder/.

Chunking Words:Read Group Of Words - My Speed Reading. (2019). https://myspeedreading.com/read-group-of-words/

Foulds, N. (2020). The benefits of NEAT - The Lean Cook. The Lean Cook. https://theleancook.com/the-benefits-of-neat/.

Improve Your Reading Speed and Comprehension. (2020). https://www.concordia.ca/content/dam/concordia/offices/cdev/docs/reading/impro

Jarrett, N. (2017). 5 Useful Accelerated Learning Techniques. https://edtech4beginners.com/2017/04/13/guest-post-5-useful-accelerated- learning-techniques/

Leech, J. (2018). 10 Health Benefits of Spirulina. Healthline. https://www.healthline.com/nutrition/10-proven-benefits-of-spirulina.

Levi, J. (2020). Is Speed Reading a Hoax? - SuperHuman Academy. https://superhumanacademy.com/podcast/is-speed-reading-a-hoax/

Multiple Intelligences: Learning from Your Strengths. (2009). https://www.learningdoorway.com/multiple-intelligences.html

Nowak, P. (2020). Speed Reading Tips: 5 Ways to Minimize Subvocalization. https://irisreading.com/speed-reading-tips-5-ways-to-minimize-subvocalization

Overview of learning styles. (2020). https://www.learning-styles-online.com/overview/

Patel, D. (2019). These 6 Types of Music Are Known to Dramatically Improve Productivity. https://www.entrepreneur.com/article/325492

Pixabay. (2020). Overcoming Stone Roll [Image]. https://pixabay.com/illustrations/overcoming-stone-roll-slide-strong-2127669/.

Pixabay. (2020). Question [Image]. https://pixabay.com/vectors/question-questions-man-head-2519654/.

Pixabay. (2020). Robot Reading Books [Image]. https://pixabay.com/illustrations/art-artwork-robot- reading-books-3569271/.

Pixabay. (2020). Vitamins [Image]. https://pixabay.com/vectors/vitamins-tablets-pills- medicine-26622/.

Rowe, K. (2020). What Are the Differences, Functions and Benefits of Omega-3, 6 &9?. BrainMD Health Blog.https://brainmd.com/blog/guide-to- omega-3-6-9-supplements/

Schiller, C. (2016). 7 science-backed tips for reading faster and retaining more. https://www.businessinsider. com/7-science-backed-tips-for- reading-faster-and-retaining-more-2016-3?IR=T#-1

Schornack, G. (2020). Accelerated Learning Techniques for Adults: An Instructional Design Concept for the Next Decade https:// www.semanticscholar.org/paper/Accelerated- Learning-Techniques-for-Adults%3A-An-for- Schornack/e1b92fedcb96e849d-f8f9f106f104ae5dad45e83

Serdyukov, P. (2008). Accelerated Learning: What is It?. https://www.researchgate.net/publication/268516488_Accelerated_Learning_What_is_

Sözüdoğru, O., & Özad, Ü. (2020). SAGE Reference - The SAGE Encyclopedia of Educational Technology.

http://sk.sagepub.com/reference/the-sage- encyclope-dia-of-educational-technology/i829.xml

Speedy History of Speed Reading. (2020). https://irisreading.com/speedy-history-of-speed-reading/#:~:text=Speed%20reading%20became% 20popular-ized%20in,many%20semi

Speed Reading: – How to Absorb Information Quickly and Effectively. (2020). https://www.mindtools.com/speedrd.html

Study Skills | Effective reading strategies. (2020). Retrieved 6 August 2020, from http://learnline.cdu.edu.au/studyskills/studyskills/ reading.html

Thornton, E. (2020). 9 incredible health benefits of omega 3. Avogel.co.uk. https://www.avogel.co.uk/food/9-incredible-health-benefits-of-omega-3/.

Trence, D. (2020). Can Vitamin B Boost My Brain Power? | Empoweryourhealth.org. Empoweryourhealth.org. https://www. empoweryourhealth.org/magazine/vol10_issue1/ can_vitamin_b_boos_

www.ingramcontent.com/pod-product-compliance
Lightning Source LLC
Chambersburg PA
CBHW021442080526
44588CB00009B/656